NUMBERS AND WORDS:

A PROBLEM PER DAY

by Marcy Cook

Cover/Illustrations by Rita Formaro

Copyright © 1987
Cuisenaire Company of America, Inc.
10 Bank Street, P.O. Box 5026, White Plains, NY 10602-5026

ISBN O-914040-52-9

INTRODUCTION

Why use *Numbers And Words: A Problem Per Day?*

Solving a word problem requires many skills. The ability to read a problem, to comprehend its meaning, and to ascertain what is being sought are all required skills for solving problems. Such skills as the ability to select numbers pertinent to the solution, to determine the operations to use, and to formulate a mathematical number sentence or equation are also necessary. Finally, it is important to be able to do the calculation and to see if the result makes sense.

It is evident that for students to get better at solving word problems, they need to solve problems. The more problem solving experience students have, the better they become at the required skills. Unfortunately, textbooks historically have presented word problems grouped according to type at the end of lessons and chapters. Once the first problem in a set is solved, the remainder require little more than the calculation. Such exercises provide more practice in computation than in problem solving.

The problems in this book, used on a daily basis, provoke the thinking skills useful in problem solving. Students have the opportunity to read, to sort out given information, to determine what is being asked, to decide how to go about getting the answer, and to see that the final result makes sense.

Who is to use *Numbers And Words: A Problem Per Day?*

The problems are appropriate for students in grades 3-8. They cover a wide range of topics, and although there is a daily theme throughout, the problems are not put in sequence according to the level of difficulty. Some of the exercises are appropriate for extension work at the early grades. Others are useful for remedial work in the later grades.

How is *Numbers And Words: A Problem Per Day* organized?

This book is designed for a school calendar of 180 days. There is a problem for each day of the week plus an additional problem which may be assigned at any time. Each day of the week has a different theme.

> Monday problems ask the student to make an estimate, always with the emphasis on how that conclusion was reached. An exact answer can be found for most problems and a comparison between this and the estimate should be encouraged.

> Tuesday problems ask the student to determine the operation(s) necessary for solving the problem. Discussion is of utmost importance since there is often more than one way to solve the problem.

> Wednesday problems ask the student to analyze the given information. Is there enough? What, if anything, is missing?

> Thursday problems ask the student to draw a picture or a diagram that would be helpful in solving the problem. Simple representation needs to be stressed rather than elaborate art work.

Friday problems ask the student to write an equation with N as the answer. By design, numbers have been omitted to prevent the student from focusing on "the answer" and then working backwards. For each problem, a hypothetical instance has been included, so that the student can check his or her equation by substituting the hypothetical amounts.

Weekly problems ask the student to insert numbers found in "cubes" into a paragraph in such a way that the paragraph will make sense. This type of problem correlates language arts and mathematics giving the student the opportunity to apply reading skills, arithmetic skills, and word problem skills to a practical situation. The paragraph makes sense only when the numbers are correctly placed.

How can the classroom teacher use *Numbers And Words: A Problem Per Day*?

One suggestion is to give a word problem each day. This can be done in a variety of ways. A problem can be written on the chalkboard, displayed on an overhead projector, posted on the bulletin board, or duplicated and distributed to each student. Another idea is to distribute all of the problems for the next week on Friday. A short discussion should follow the assignment of each problem to be sure that it is understood. Then the students could consider the problems individually, with a partner, or in small groups.

When discussing the solutions to the problems, students should be encouraged to tell how they reached their conclusions. Many different avenues of thought are possible and no one is more correct than another. Several discussion questions are suggested below.

How can you attack this problem?
What do you conclude? Why?
How can you decide that?
Will the result always be the same?
What assumptions, if any, can you make?
Why does that make sense to you?

Estimate . . . On the average, how many hours per week is the television set "on" in American homes?

Tuesday

How many inches are in five feet?

Do you add, subtract, multiply, or divide?

Wednesday

A basketball team has five players. Only three scored in today's game. One player made 16 points, while each of the other two made double that amount. How many points were scored in today's game?

Can you solve this problem? If not, what do you need to know?

Thursday

In a parking lot, five cars are parked in a row. If there are seven rows just like this, how many cars are parked in the lot?

Draw a diagram to show your answer.

Friday

If one gallon of lemonade will serve ☐ people, how many people will five gallons serve?

Write the equation. Let N stand for the answer.

(If one gallon serves 20 people, can you solve the equation?)

Numbers And Words: A Problem Per Day © 1987 Cuisenaire Company of America, Inc.

Weekly

Place each number below in one of the blanks to create the most meaningful and realistic story possible.

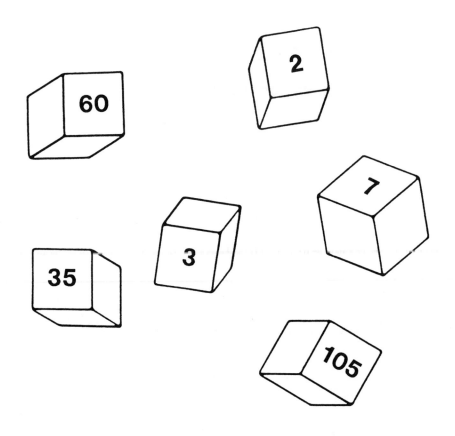

_____ classes of _____ students each are going on a field trip together. Since each school bus can hold _____ passengers, _____ buses are needed to hold the _____ students and _____ adults who are going with the children.

Numbers And Words: A Problem Per Day © 1987 Cuisenaire Company Of America, Inc.

Monday

Estimate . . . How many meters high is the ceiling of your classroom?

Tuesday

How many more coins does your mother have than you?

Do you add, subtract, multiply, or divide?

Wednesday

Three drinks and one hamburger cost a total of $3.00. What is the cost of one drink?

Can you solve this problem? If not, what do you need to know?

Thursday

An empty barrel can hold 16 quarts of water. It is only half full when I add 2 quarts of water and my brother adds 5 quarts. How many quarts of water are now in the barrel?

Draw a diagram to show your answer.

Friday

It takes 4 hours to repair my computer. Labor costs $ ☐ per hour. The parts cost $95. What is the total cost of repairing my computer?

Write the equation. Let N stand for the answer.

(If labor costs $25 per hour, can you solve the equation?)

Numbers And Words: A Problem Per Day © 1987 Cuisenaire Company of America, Inc.

Weekly

Place each number below in one of the blanks to create the most meaningful and realistic story possible.

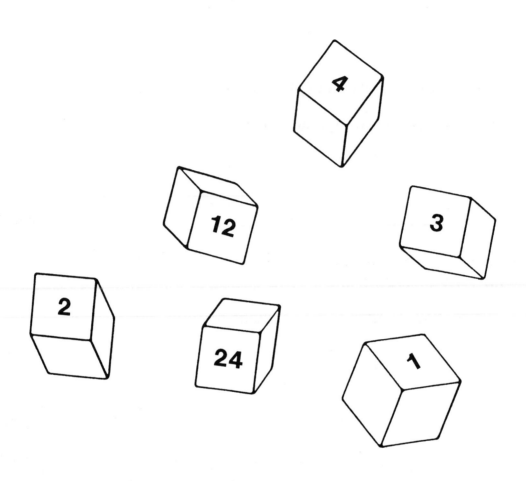

At dinner we usually set out _____ items of silverware (a fork, a knife, and a spoon) for each person. If there are _____ people, we will need _____ pieces of silverware. If each person also uses _____ plates and _____ glass, I will have to wash _____ items tonight.

Monday

Estimate . . . How many birthday twins do you have in your class? (Birthday twins have birthdays on the same month and same day. The year may be different).

Tuesday

If it takes you one hour to do your chores each day, how many hours do you spend doing chores in one month?

Do you add, subtract, multiply, or divide?

Wednesday

Tara leaves for school at 8:00 a.m. If snack time is 2 hours before lunch, what time does Tara eat?

Can you solve this problem? If not, what do you need to know?

Thursday

Casey is packing a box of 24 candies. He puts 4 candies in each row. How many rows of candy will he make?

Draw a diagram to show your answer.

Friday

Bev, Nancy, and Lynn each have ☐ posters. How many do they have altogether?

Write the equation. Let N stand for the answer.

(If they each have 5 posters, can you solve the equation?)

Weekly

Place each number below in one of the blanks to create the most meaningful and realistic story possible.

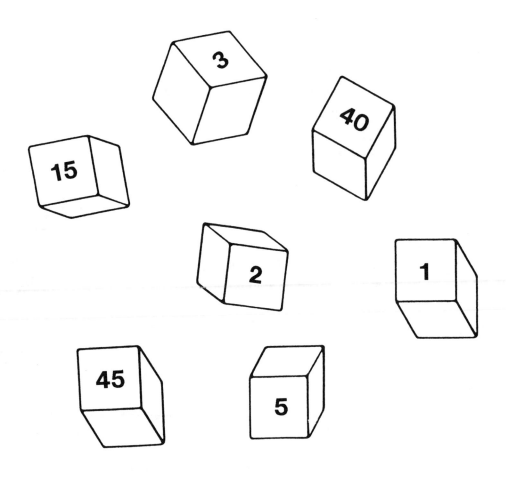

I am buying _____ items for _____ cents and _____ cents. I give the clerk a _____ dollar bill. Since he needs to give me _____ cents change, he must give me _____ coins worth _____ cents each.

Numbers And Words: A Problem Per Day ©1987 Cuisenaire Company Of America, Inc.

Estimate . . How many sections are in an orange?

A farmer gathers more than six dozen eggs from the hen house. He sells the eggs for 79¢ a dozen. How much money does he make from selling the eggs?

Do you add, subtract, multiply, or divide?

A spelling test has 100 words. The correct spelling of 90 words or more earns an A. Anne receives an A. How many words does she spell correctly?

Can you solve this problem? If not, what do you need to know?

There are three rows of nine squares each. Each row starts and ends with a black square. All of the other squares are white. How many squares are black and how many are white?

Draw a diagram to show your answer.

I have ☐ dollars. If I buy a tape for $8.00 and candy for $1.50, how much do I now have?

Write the equation. Let N stand for the answer.

(If I have $10, can you solve the equation?)

Numbers And Words: A Problem Per Day © 1987 Cuisenaire Company of America, Inc.

Weekly

Place each number below in one of the blanks to create the most meaningful and realistic story possible.

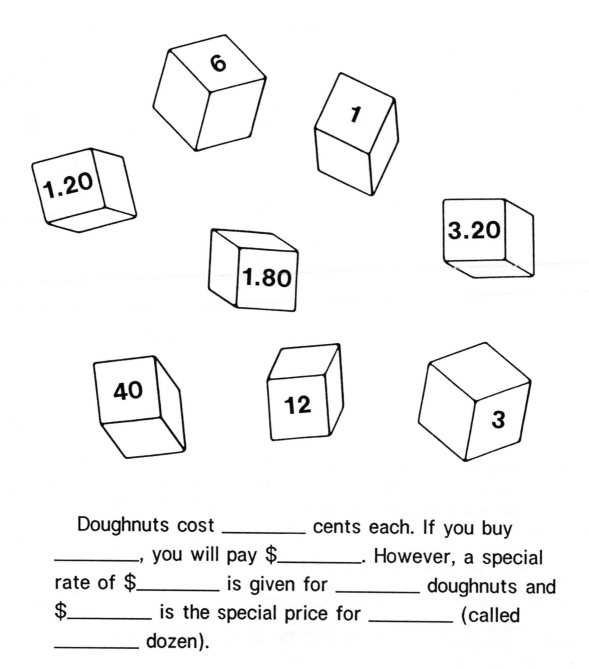

Doughnuts cost _____ cents each. If you buy _____, you will pay $_____. However, a special rate of $_____ is given for _____ doughnuts and $_____ is the special price for _____ (called _____ dozen).

Numbers And Words: A Problem Per Day © 1987 Cuisenaire Company Of America, Inc.

Estimate . . . How many years of your life have you spent sleeping?

All 44 members of the football team are at an awards dinner. Half of the team brought their dads. How many people are at the dinner?

Do you add, subtract, multiply, or divide?

How many shoelaces long is your chalkboard?

Can you solve this problem? If not, what do you need to know?

A log is eight feet long. I want to cut it into pieces that are each one foot long. How many cuts must I make?

Draw a diagram to show your answer.

Dad has a roll of 100 stamps. He needs ☐ stamps to pay the bills. How many stamps will he have left?

Write the equation. Let N stand for the answer.

(If he uses 16 stamps, can you solve the equation?)

Weekly

Place each number below in one of the blanks to create the most meaningful and realistic story possible.

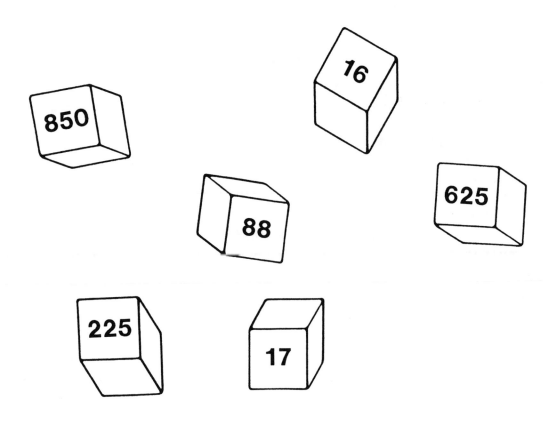

Most of the people in a town whose population is _____ have listed phone numbers. Of the _____ listed numbers, only a half dozen end in the double digit number _____. Of the _____ unlisted numbers, only _____ end in the odd number _____.

Monday

Estimate . . . How many pennies weigh one pound?

Tuesday

My french toast cost $1.49 while my mom's pancakes cost $2.99. My milk is 50¢ and her coffee is 60¢. What is the cost of our meal?

Do you add, subtract, multiply, or divide?

Wednesday

A test has 30 questions on it. Bob scores 100%. How many questions does he get wrong?

Can you solve this problem? If not, what do you need to know?

Thursday

A motorboat travels 25 miles in the time a sailboat travels 10 miles. At this rate, how far will the motorboat travel when the sailboat has traveled 60 miles?

Draw a diagram to show your answer.

Friday

If I feed my cats ☐ cans of cat food every day in April, how many cans will I need that month?

Write the equation. Let N stand for the answer.

(If I use 2 cans each day, can you solve the equation?)

Numbers And Words: A Problem Per Day ©1987 Cuisenaire Company of America,

Weekly

Place each number below in one of the blanks to create the most meaningful and realistic story possible.

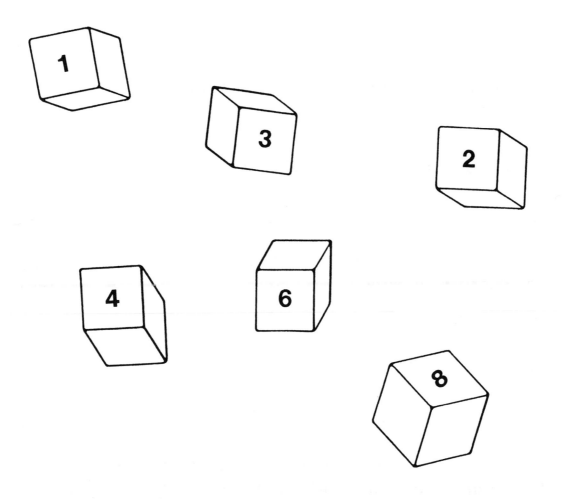

A recipe calls for 4 cups of flour, _____ tablespoons of sugar, and 2 eggs. If I double the recipe I will need _____ cups of flour, _____ tablespoons of sugar, and _____ eggs. However, if I only make half the recipe I will use _____ cups of flour, 1 1/2 tablespoons of sugar, and _____ egg.

Monday

Estimate . . . How many horizontal lines are on one side of an 8½" x 11" piece of notebook paper?

Tuesday

How many vans does your class need if a dozen students can fit into one van?

Do you add, subtract, multiply, or divide?

Wednesday

Laura will turn 18 next May. Her sister, who is 2 years younger, also has her birthday in May. How old will Laura's sister be next April?

Can you solve this problem? If not, what do you need to know?

Thursday

You have 5 squares and 4 circles. Each square has 3 dots inside, while each circle has 4 dots inside. How many dots are inside all the figures?

Draw a diagram to show your answer.

Friday

Steve is taking a test with ☐ questions. If he misses six, how many will he answer correctly?

Write the equation. Let N stand for the answer.

(If there are 65 questions on the test, can you solve the equation?)

Numbers And Words: A Problem Per Day © 1987 Cuisenaire Company of America, Inc.

Weekly

Place each number below in one of the blanks to create the most meaningful and realistic story possible.

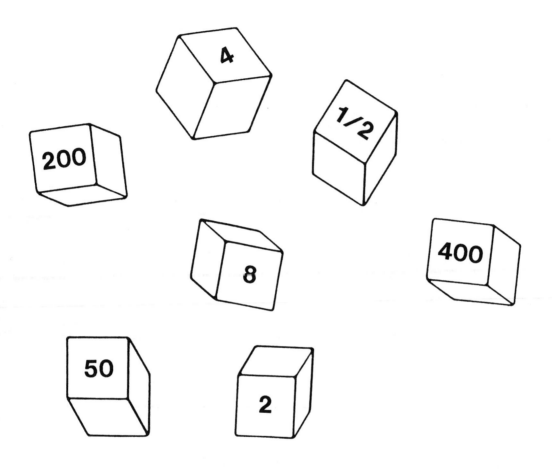

The distance between _____ towns is _____ miles. If I travel a little slower than the speed limit, _____ miles per hour, it will take me about _____ hours to get _____ way or _____ miles. At that rate, it would take me _____ hours to travel the entire distance.

Estimate . . . How many shoelace holes are in your classroom today?

A local department store opened in 1924. How long has it been in business?

Do you add, subtract, multiply, or divide?

Four containers of pudding cost 99¢. How much will 12 containers of pudding cost?

Can you solve this problem? If not, what do you need to know?

Sixty men are standing in a line. The first man steps forward, the second man steps back, the third man steps forward, the fourth man steps back, and so on. If they continue in this manner, what will the thirtieth man do?

Draw a diagram to show your answer.

Pencils cost ▢ ¢ each. If I buy a dozen of them, how much will I spend?

Write the equation. Let N stand for the answer.

(If pencils cost 12¢ each, can you solve the equation?)

Weekly

Place each number below in one of the blanks to create the most meaningful and realistic story possible.

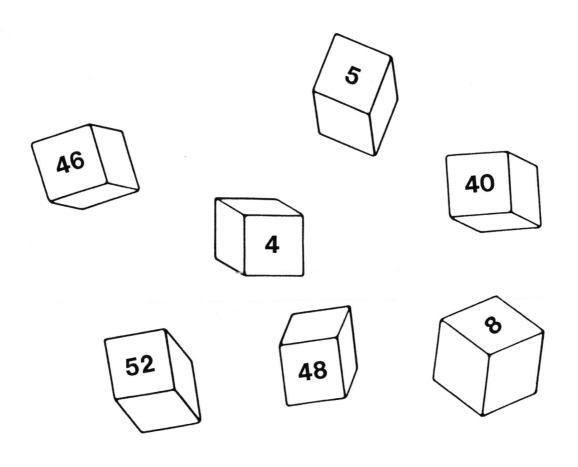

Many people work _____ days a week, _____ hours a day, for a total of _____ hours a week. If they get _____ weeks of vacation in the summer, they work about _____ weeks a year. If they also get two weeks for winter vacation, they only work _____ of the _____ weeks.

Monday

Estimate . . . How many miles long (north to south) is the state in which you live?

Tuesday

On a business trip, Mr. Speed drives his car 80 miles each way. If his car can go 20 miles on one gallon of gas, how many gallons of gas does Mr. Speed need for the round trip?

Do you add, subtract, multiply, or divide?

Wednesday

Two orange drinks cost $1.00 while 2 malts cost $2.20. If I buy one orange drink and one malt, how much will I pay?

Can you solve this problem? If not, what do you need to know?

Thursday

There are 15 apples on the table. Three children want to share them equally. How many apples will each child get?

Draw a diagram to show your answer.

Friday

Kevin's mom is ☐ years old. Kevin is 13 years old. How much older than Kevin is his mom?

Write the equation. Let N stand for the answer.

(If Kevin's mom is 39, can you solve the equation?)

Numbers And Words: A Problem Per Day ©1987 Cuisenaire Company of America, Inc.

Weekly

Place each number below in one of the blanks to create the most meaningful and realistic story possible.

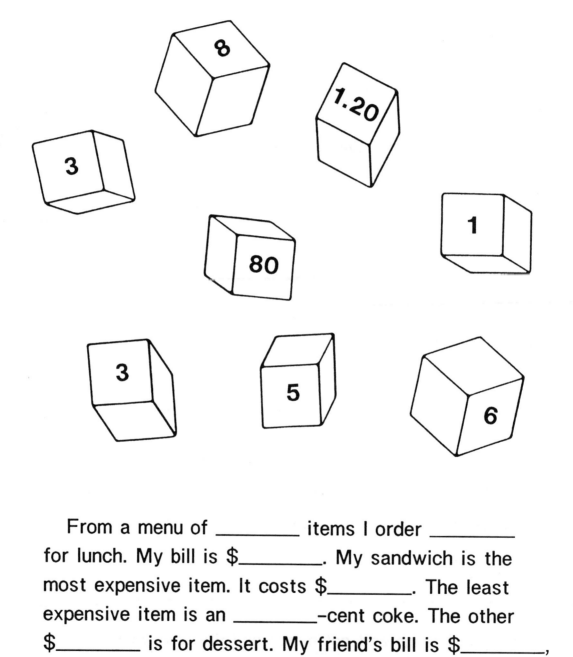

From a menu of _____ items I order _____ for lunch. My bill is $_____. My sandwich is the most expensive item. It costs $_____. The least expensive item is an _____-cent coke. The other $_____ is for dessert. My friend's bill is $_____, exactly $_____ more than mine.

Monday

Estimate . . . How many bones are in your two arms?
(A person has 206 bones in all.)

Tuesday

The Rent-A-Wreck Company charges $33 a day to rent
a car. The Drive-Away Company charges $69 per day.
How much can you save by renting a car from the
Rent-A-Wreck Company?

Do you add, subtract, multiply, or divide?

Wednesday

If Jan takes two minutes to read a full page in her reader,
how long will it take her to read the entire book of 320
pages?

**Can you solve this problem? If not, what do you need
to know?**

Thursday

Jackie has an orange. She eats half of it at lunch. For
a snack, she eats half of the half that was not eaten. How
much orange does she have left?

Draw a diagram to show your answer.

Friday

Terry works five days a week for ☐ weeks. How many
days does he work?

Write the equation. Let N stand for the answer.

(If he works for 8 weeks, can you solve the equation?)

Numbers And Words: A Problem Per Day © 1987 Cuisenaire Company of America, Inc.

Weekly

Place each number below in one of the blanks to create the most meaningful and realistic story possible.

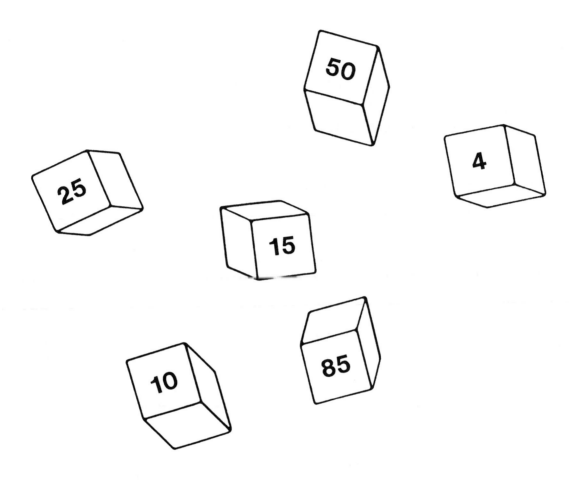

Jan didn't know how to spend her 100 pennies. She could have bought _____ jawbreakers for a dime each or _____ candy bars at _____ cents each or 2 cookies at _____ cents each. If she bought 1 jawbreaker, 1 candy bar and 1 cookie she would spend _____ cents and still have _____ cents left.

Estimate . . . How many days are between Valentine's Day and the Fourth of July?

Tuesday

If you can buy five candy bars for one dollar, how much will you pay for three candy bars?

Do you add, subtract, multiply, or divide?

Wednesday

Duane grew two inches this year while Joe only grew one inch. Duane is now 49 inches tall. How tall is Joe?

Can you solve this problem? If not, what do you need to know?

Thursday

Mom has four meat pies. She wants to cut them so each of the six people have the same amount. What is the size of each piece?

Draw a diagram to show your answer.

Friday

I have $256 in the bank. If I deposit $ ☐ , how much will I have in the bank?

Write the equation. Let N stand for the answer.

(If I deposit $43, can you solve the equation?)

Numbers And Words: A Problem Per Day © 1987 Cuisenaire Company of America, Inc.

Weekly

Place each number below in one of the blanks to create the most meaningful and realistic story possible.

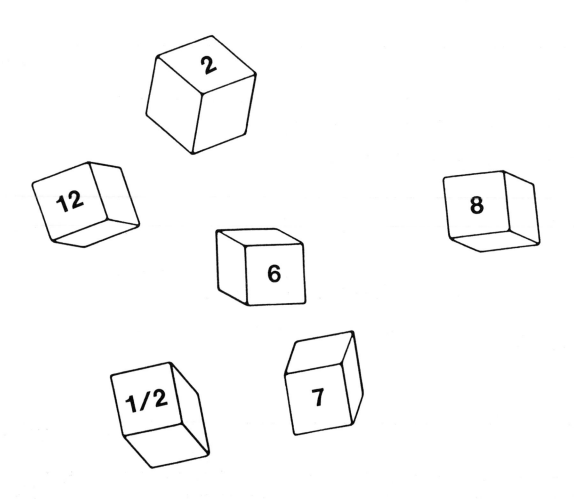

My pencil is _____ inches long, which is more than _____ the length of my _____-inch ruler. My eraser is only _____ inches long. The chalkboard eraser is _____ inches, which is one inch longer than my pencil. After I sharpen my pencil, it will be about _____ inches long.

Estimate . . . How many capital letters of the alphabet can be drawn without lifting your pencil or retracing?

A piece of gum costs 5¢. I buy 27 pieces of gum. How much do I pay?

Do you add, subtract, multiply, or divide?

Bus tour prices range from $499 to $2099. How much more will you pay for the most expensive bus tour than for the least expensive one?

Can you solve this problem? If not, what do you need to know?

A tray is 6" long by 4" wide. How may dominoes will fit in the tray if each domino is 2" long and 1" wide?

Draw a diagram to show your answer.

Ruth had ☐ plants. Today at the nursery she bought a dozen more. How many plants does she now have?

Write the equation. Let N stand for the answer.

(If she had 18 plants, can you solve the equation?)

Numbers And Words: A Problem Per Day © 1987 Cuisenaire Company of America, Inc.

Weekly

Place each number below in one of the blanks to create the most meaningful and realistic story possible.

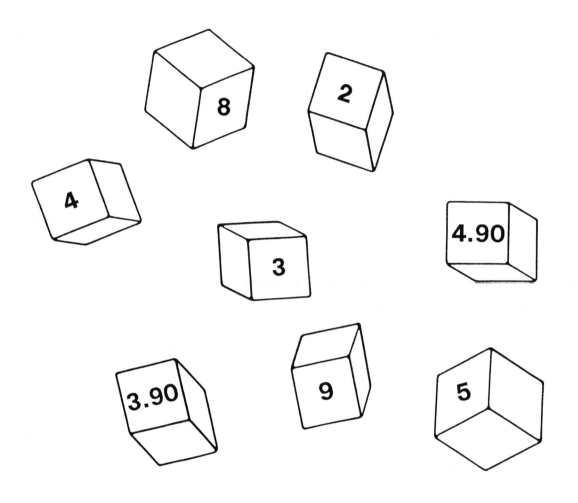

For lunch Bob orders _____ items which come to a total of $_____. Jim's order of $_____ is more than Bob's since he is ordering _____ more items than Bob. The total for the _____ items is about $_____ with Bob's share about $_____ and Jim's share about $_____.

Numbers And Words: A Problem Per Day © 1987 Cuisenaire Company Of America, Inc.

Estimate . . . What percent of the capital letters of the alphabet are formed with straight lines only?

Everyone in your class will get 2 cookies today. How many cookies are needed?

Do you add, subtract, multiply, or divide?

Eric washes cars for $2.00 each. If he washes one Ford, two Audis, and three Nissans today, how much money will he earn?

Can you solve this problem? If not, what do you need to know?

There are six bunches of bananas with 5 bananas in each bunch. How many bananas are there?

Draw a diagram to show your answer.

It is 30 miles from my house to Judy's house. It is ☐ miles further to Trudy's house. How far is it from my house to Trudy's?

Write the equation. Let N stand for the answer.

(If it is 10 miles further to Trudy's house, can you solve the equation?)

Weekly

Place each number below in one of the blanks to create the most meaningful and realistic story possible.

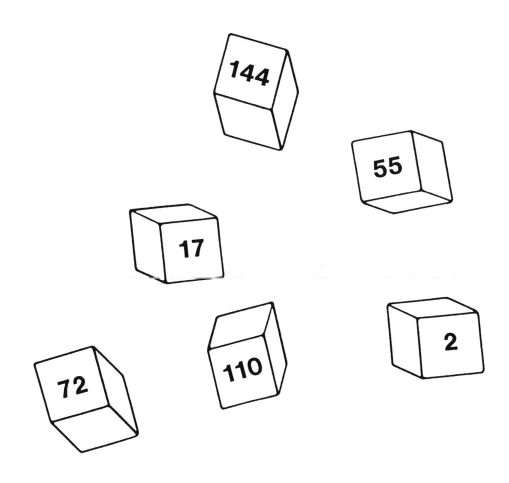

A car going _____ miles per hour exceeds the _____ mph speed limit by _____ miles per hour. If the car travels _____ hours at the higher speed, it will cover _____ miles rather than _____ miles at the posted speed limit.

Estimate . . . How many of your math books will stack
to make a pile one meter high?

Jill gets a ticket for speeding. She exceeded the limit by
10 miles per hour. She has to pay $5.00 for each mile
over the speed limit. How much must she pay?

Do you add, subtract, multiply, or divide?

A small hotel has 44 rooms. Each room has the same
number of beds. How many beds are in the hotel?

**Can you solve this problem? If not, what do you need
to know?**

A square yard has a fence around it. Each corner has
a post. Each side of the yard has 4 posts in all. How many
posts are around this yard?

Draw a diagram to show your answer.

Jim is buying a surfboard on sale for $85. He will pay
$ ☐ less than the original price. How much was the
original price?

Write the equation. Let N stand for the answer.

(If he paid $20 less than the original price, can you solve
the equation?)

Weekly

Place each number below in one of the blanks to create the most meaningful and realistic story possible.

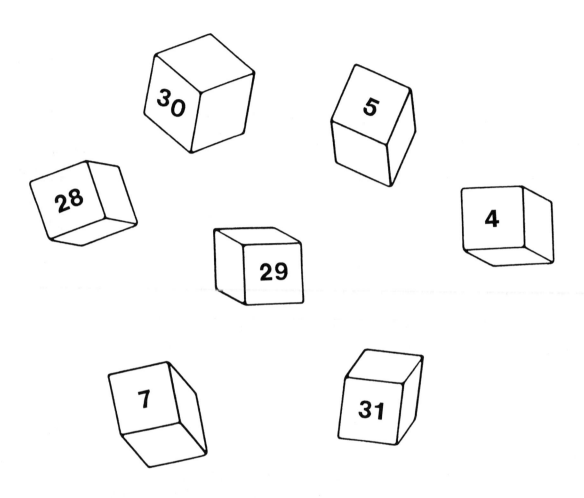

My birthday is in a month with _____ days. It follows a month which has _____ or _____ days. The month after my birthday has _____ days. The date of my birth is a single odd digit, _____. Almost exactly _____ months after my birthday is a major holiday in the United States. It is in the _____th month and is usually celebrated with fireworks.

Numbers And Words: A Problem Per Day ©1987 Cuisenaire Company Of America, Inc.

Monday

Estimate . . . Which letter of the alphabet is used most often?

Tuesday

If it takes about 8 apples to make a pie, how many pies can you make with 100 apples?

Do you add, subtract, multiply, or divide?

Wednesday

Three chocolate bars, each weighing 3 ounces, cost a total of 90¢. How much do two of these candy bars cost?

Can you solve this problem? If not, what do you need to know?

Thursday

A farmer plants three rows of corn. She puts six plants in each row. How many corn plants does she have?

Draw a diagram to show your answer.

Friday

Mom baked ☐ cookies. She gave half of them to the PTA. How many did she give to the PTA?

Write the equation. Let N stand for the answer.

(If she baked 90 cookies, can you solve the equation?)

Numbers And Words: A Problem Per Day © 1987 Cuisenaire Company of America, Inc.

Weekly

Place each number below in one of the blanks to create the most meaningful and realistic story possible.

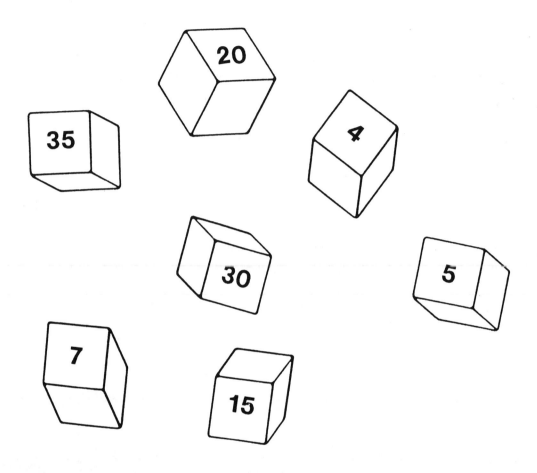

For the holidays I received $_____ in gift money. Half a dozen model cars will cost _____. Since I have $_____ more than that, I could buy _____ models. If I only buy _____ models, my bill would be $_____ and I would still have $_____ left.

Monday

Estimate . . . How many square feet of chalkboard space do you have in your classroom?

Tuesday

If a plane averages 406 miles per hour, how many hours will it take to fly 1,015 miles?

Do you add, subtract, multiply, or divide?

Wednesday

Eight people are at a picnic. Each person eats two hamburgers. What is the total number of hamburgers eaten?

Can you solve this problem? If not, what do you need to know?

Thursday

A dodge ball circle is divided in half. Each half is divided in half. Each of these new areas is divided in half. How many equal areas are there?

Draw a diagram to show your answer.

Friday

Casey has two model planes and ☐ model ships. He also has twice as many model cars as he has model planes. How many models does he have altogether?

Write the equation. Let N stand for the answer.

(If he has 7 model ships, can you solve the equation?)

Numbers And Words: A Problem Per Day © 1987 Cuisenaire Company of America, Inc.

Place each number below in one of the blanks to create the most meaningful and realistic story possible.

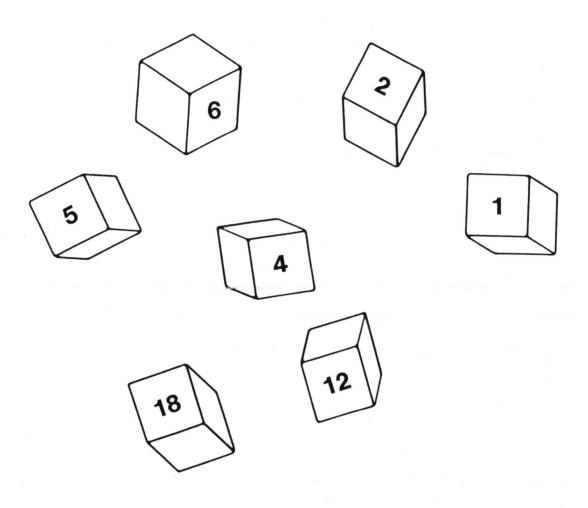

A dog had 3 litters of puppies with _____ puppies in each litter. Of the _____ puppies, there were 6 males and _____ females. In the first litter, _____ were males and _____ were females. In the second litter, the number of males was equal to the number of females. In the third litter, there was _____ male and _____ females.

Estimate . . . How many states in the U.S.A. begin with a letter in the first half of our alphabet?

Regular gas costs 99¢ per gallon. Unleaded gas costs $1.15 per gallon. If I buy 15 gallons of gas, how much more will I pay for unleaded than regular?

Do you add, subtract, multiply, or divide?

A store opens at 9 A.M. and closes at the end of the day. How many hours a day is the store open?

Can you solve this problem? If not, what do you need to know?

Four crayons (red, blue, yellow, and green) are placed in a row. How many different ways can they be placed?

Draw a diagram to show your answer.

Ninety students are placed equally on ☐ teams for gym. How many students are on each team?

Write the equation. Let N stand for the answer.

(If there are 10 teams, can you solve the equation?)

Numbers And Words: A Problem Per Day © 1987 Cuisenaire Company of America, Inc.

Place each number below in one of the blanks to create the most meaningful and realistic story possible.

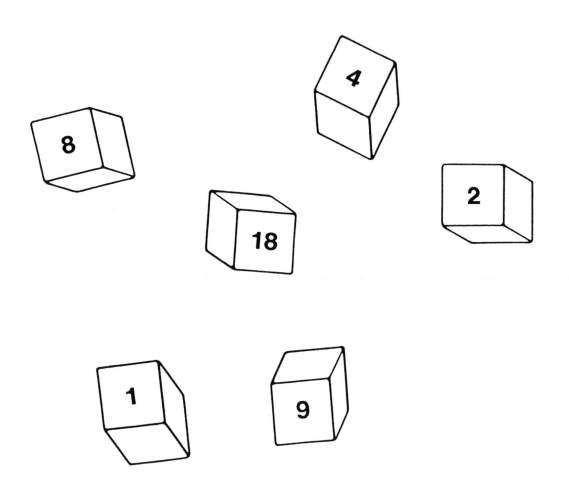

The sum of the digits in my four-digit address is _____. The largest digit is an _____ and is at the end of the number. The smallest digit is a _____ and is at the beginning. If I add the middle _____ digits I get the same sum as if I add the end digits. This sum, _____, is half the sum of the whole address. The third number, which is _____, is half of the fourth number.

Estimate . . . If each person were to add up the digits of his/her phone number, what would be the most common sum?

Matt and Mike ran a race. Matt ran it in 58.3 seconds. Mike ran it in 59.8 seconds. Who won and by how many seconds?

Do you add, subtract, multiply, or divide?

Debbie writes two checks, one for $5.30 and one for $7.42. How much money does she have left in her account?

Can you solve this problem? If not, what do you need to know?

A rectangular field is 9' x 12'. A fence cuts the area into two smaller rectangles which are the same size. If the perimeter of each of these smaller rectangles is 30 feet, what is the length and width of each rectangle?

Draw a diagram to show your answer.

One cake serves 12 people. If I know ☐ people will be at my party, how many cakes should I buy?

Write the equation. Let N stand for the answer.

(If 48 people will be at my party, can you solve the equation?)

Weekly

Place each number below in one of the blanks to create the most meaningful and realistic story possible.

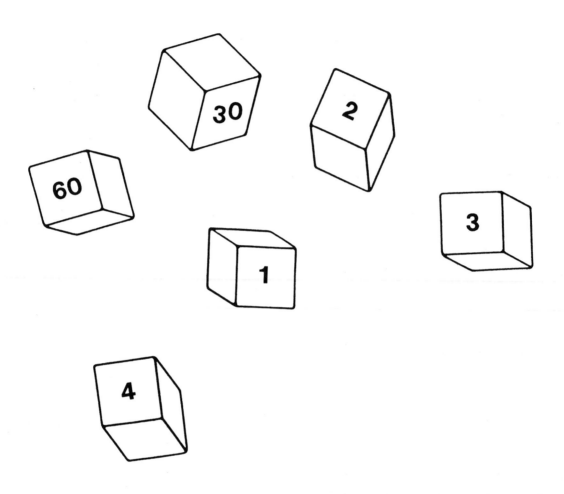

If I can run _____ miles in _____ minutes, I should be able to run _____ miles in _____ hour. However, due to tiring, I usually walk briskly and can cover about _____ miles in a _____-minute period of time.

Estimate . . . How many seconds can most people stand still on one foot with no support and their eyes closed?

Bob wants to buy three computer programs. The first costs $28, the second costs $35, and the third costs $49. How much money will he spend on all three programs?

Do you add, subtract, multiply, or divide?

John is 5'2" tall. George is 2" shorter than John. Jerry is the tallest. How tall is George?

Can you solve this problem? If not, what do you need to know?

Twenty marbles are equally divided among four people. How many marbles does each person get?

Draw a diagram to show your answer.

Five students in our class have ☐ dogs each. How many dogs do these students have altogether?

Write the equation. Let N stand for the answer.

(If each student has 3 dogs, can you solve the equation?)

Weekly

Place each number below in one of the blanks to create the most meaningful and realistic story possible.

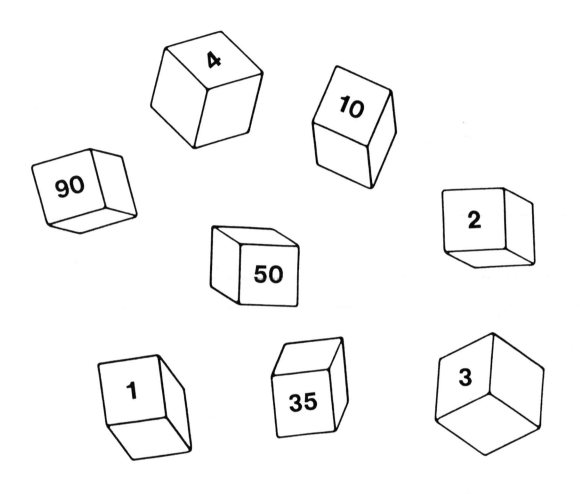

Sarita buys 4 rolls at _____ cents each, _____ mixes at 25 cents each, _____ containers of milk at _____ dollar each and a loaf of bread for _____ cents. She gives the clerk a _____-dollar bill. She receives _____ dollars and _____ cents in change.

Monday

Estimate . . . What is the population of the city or town in which you live?

Tuesday

Six cans of soda costs $2.49. If you buy 48 cans, how much will you pay?

Do you add, subtract, multiply, or divide?

Wednesday

I bought three pairs of shoes yesterday and two pairs today. How many pairs of shoes do I now own?

Can you solve this problem? If not, what do you need to know?

Thursday

Each flower has three petals. How many petals will seven flowers have?

Draw a diagram to show your answer.

Friday

Bob is mailing ☐ letters. Each letter requires 22¢ postage. How much does the postage cost?

Write the equation. Let N stand for the answer.

(If he mails 4 letters, can you solve the equation?)

Numbers And Words: A Problem Per Day © 1987 Cuisenaire Company of America, Inc.

Weekly

Place each number below in one of the blanks to create the most meaningful and realistic story possible.

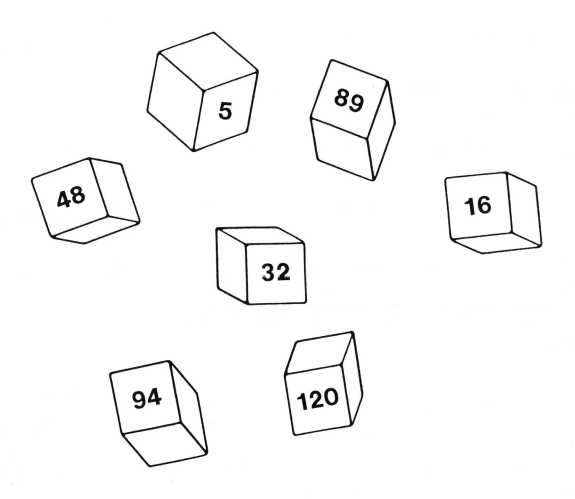

The high temperature yesterday was _____ degrees Fahrenheit, the highest it has been for the past _____ days. The low temperature was _____ degrees Fahrenheit, about half the high, and only _____ degrees above freezing, (which is _____ degrees Fahrenheit). Tomorrow's temperature is predicted to be _____ degrees Fahrenheit, which is _____ degrees lower than yesterday's high.

Numbers And Words: A Problem Per Day © 1987 Cuisenaire Company Of America, Inc.

Estimate . . . What percent of the students in your grade are left-handed?

Nineteen birds were in a tree. A whistle blew and frightened away some of the birds. How many remained in the tree?

Do you add, subtract, multiply, or divide?

The 30 students in Mrs. Keye's class are put into 3 reading groups. How many are in each group?

Can you solve this problem? If not, what do you need to know?

Elaine has three skirts and four blouses. How many outfits can she make by using different blouses with each skirt?

Draw a diagram to show your answer.

Don drives 480 miles in 2 days. If he drives ☐ miles the first day, how many miles must he drive the second day?

Write the equation. Let N stand for the answer.

(If he drives 250 miles the first day, can you solve the equation?)

Weekly

Place each number below in one of the blanks to create the most meaningful and realistic story possible.

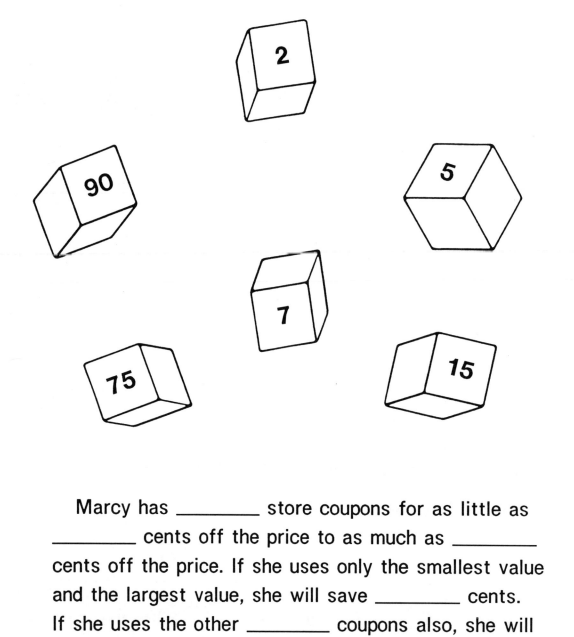

Marcy has _____ store coupons for as little as _____ cents off the price to as much as _____ cents off the price. If she uses only the smallest value and the largest value, she will save _____ cents. If she uses the other _____ coupons also, she will save over _____ dollars.

Monday

Estimate . . . How many times does "1" or "one" appear on a dollar bill, excluding the serial number?

Tuesday

Four people eat lunch together. Each one has an 89¢-hamburger, a 35¢-drink, and a 49¢-order of french fries. What is the total bill?

Do you add, subtract, multiply, or divide?

Wednesday

How many donuts do I have if I purchase four dozen donuts?

Can you solve this problem? If not, what do you need to know?

Thursday

The teacher asks her 32 students to sit at tables with 4 students per table. How many tables does she have?

Draw a diagram to show your answer.

Friday

Three hundred cattle are put in ☐ corrals. How many cattle are in each corral, if the same number is put in each corral?

Write the equation. Let N stand for the answer.

(If there are 3 corrals, can you solve the equation?)

Numbers And Words: A Problem Per Day © 1987 Cuisenaire Company of America, Inc.

Weekly

Place each number below in one of the blanks to create the most meaningful and realistic story possible.

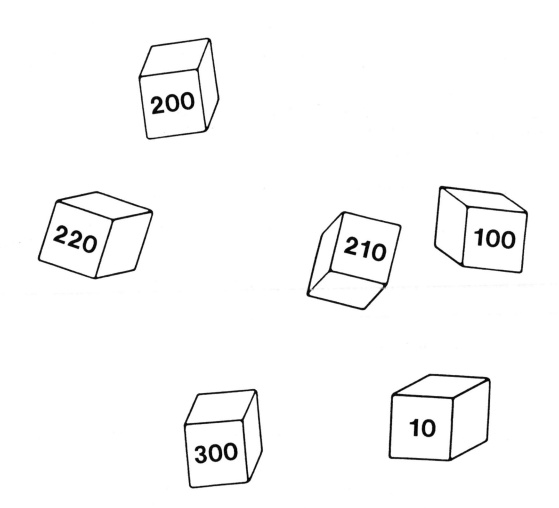

In bowling there are _____ frames per game with a maximum of 30 points per frame. A perfect score is _____ points. If I bowled games of 180, _____, 190, and _____ I would have an average of _____, which is _____ points below the perfect score.

Monday

Estimate . . . How many passenger seats are on a 747 airplane?

Tuesday

Seventeen scouts are going to see a play. Five mothers are going with them. How many are going to the play?

Do you add, subtract, multiply, or divide?

Wednesday

Potatoes cost 40¢ a pound. I pay 80¢ for four potatoes. How much does one potato weigh? How much does one potato cost?

Can you solve this problem? If not, what do you need to know?

Thursday

From Center Street, Elm Street is 2½ miles west, while Maple Street is 1½ miles east. How far is it from Elm Street to Maple Street?

Draw a diagram to show your answer.

Friday

I have 2 cookies. Liz has 3 more than I do. Cindy has ☐ cookies. How many cookies do we have in all?

Write the equation. Let N stand for the answer.

(If Cindy has half a dozen cookies, can you solve the equation?)

Weekly

Place each number below in one of the blanks to create the most meaningful and realistic story possible.

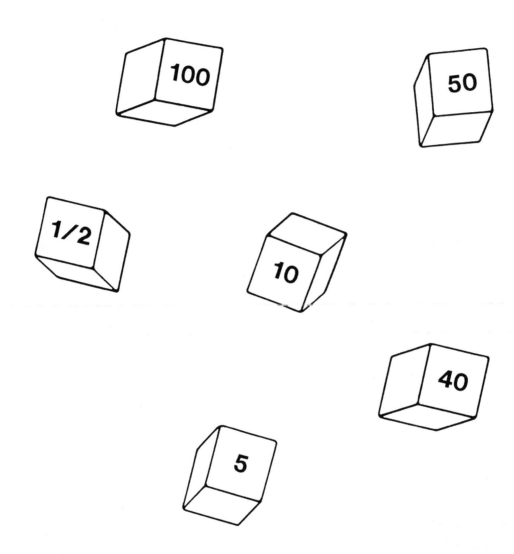

A room may be measured in terms of length and width. If the room is a square with _____ feet on each side, it has an area of _____ square feet. The distance around the room is _____ feet. If I carpet only _____ of the room, I can use a piece of carpet 10 feet long by _____ feet wide (an area of _____ square feet).

Monday

Estimate . . . How many times does a newborn baby's pulse beat per minute if a 10 year-old's pulse rate is 87?

Tuesday

If you use the computer two hours every day, how many hours will you use it in a year?

Do you add, subtract, multiply, or divide?

Wednesday

A family of five went on a trip together. They had 10 pieces of luggage in all. How many pieces of luggage did each member of the family pack?

Can you solve this problem? If not, what do you need to know?

Thursday

A rectangular-shaped building has four windows on each of the longer sides and half that many on each of the shorter sides. How many windows does this building have?

Draw a diagram to show your answer.

Friday

I need ☐ dozen cupcakes for the party. How many cupcakes do I need?

Write the equation. Let N stand for the answer.

(If I need 3 dozen cupcakes, can you solve the equation?)

Weekly

Place each number below in one of the blanks to create the most meaningful and realistic story possible.

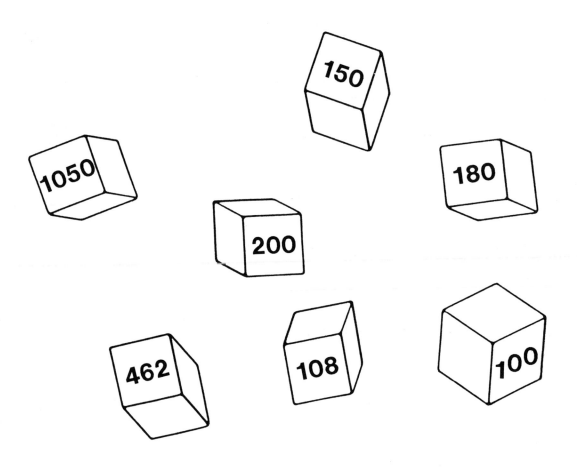

This week a bookstore sold a total of _____ books, an average of _____ books each day. The high sales day of _____ was twice the amount of the low sales day of _____. On the second lowest sales day, _____ books were sold, while _____ were sold on the second highest sales day. The books sold on the other days added up to _____.

Estimate . . . What is your average caloric intake per day?

Bananas cost 39¢ a pound. I spend $1.95 on bananas. How many pounds of bananas do I buy?

Do you add, subtract, multiply, or divide?

One ladder has 12 steps. Another has 8 steps. How many feet longer is the 12-step ladder than the 8-step ladder?

Can you solve this problem? If not, what do you need to know?

A train travels 30 miles in 10 minutes. How far will it travel in 50 minutes?

Draw a diagram to show your answer.

The teacher wants to seat his ☐ children in 4 rows, so each row has the same number of children. How many children will be in each row?

Write the equation. Let N stand for the answer.

(If there are 28 children, can you solve the equation?)

Weekly

Place each number below in one of the blanks to create the most meaningful and realistic story possible.

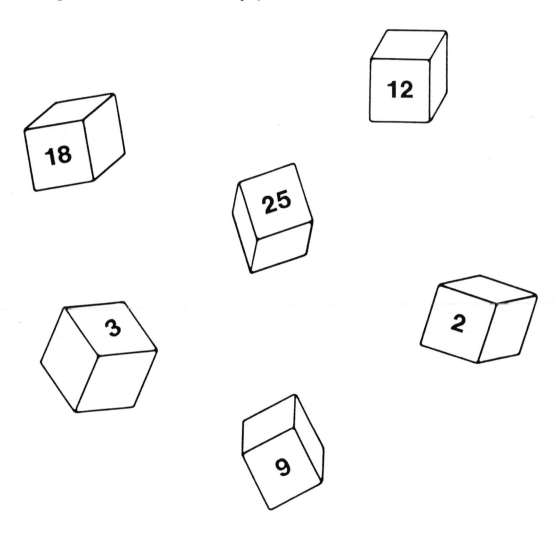

A magazine subscription of $_____ a year is reduced to $_____. This is a savings of $_____, which is _____% off the regular price. If I buy _____ subscriptions this year, I will pay $_____.

Numbers And Words: A Problem Per Day ©1987 Cuisenaire Company Of America, Inc.

Monday

Estimate . . . How many steps are in the Empire State Building which is 102 stories high?

Tuesday

How many cents are in $3.00?

Do you add, subtract, multiply, or divide?

Wednesday

Marilyn is buying a candy bar for 35¢. She gives the storekeeper one dollar. How many quarters, at most, will she receive in her change?

Can you solve this problem? If not, what do you need to know?

Thursday

I ate half of the apple pie. My brother ate a quarter of the pie. How much of the pie is left?

Draw a diagram to show your answer.

Friday

I usually wear 5 necklaces. Today I am only wearing ☐ of them. How many less than usual am I wearing today?

Write the equation. Let N stand for the answer.

(If I am wearing 2 necklaces today, can you solve the equation?)

Numbers And Words: A Problem Per Day © 1987 Cuisenaire Company of America, Inc.

Weekly

Place each number below in one of the blanks to create the most meaningful and realistic story possible.

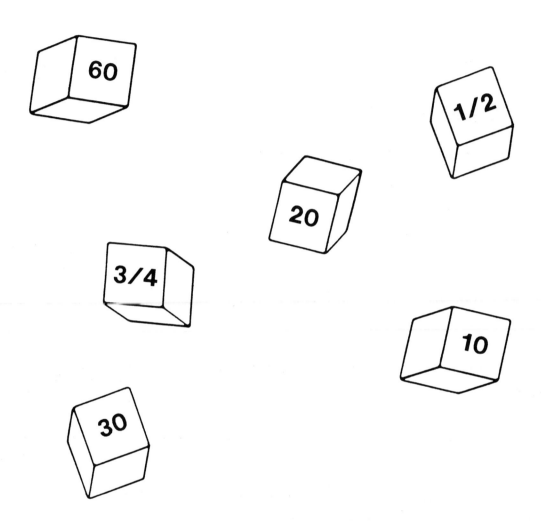

Kevin takes _____ minutes to mow the lawn while his brother can do it in half the time, _____ minutes. If they both work at their respective rates for _____ minutes, they will finish the job. If they work together for _____ minutes, they will only complete _____ the job. If they work together for 5 minutes, only a quarter of the job would be done with _____ left to do.

Estimate . . . How many numbers between 0 and 100 are formed with straight lines only?

Together Ted and Paul have read a total of 108 books. If Paul has read 68 books, how many more books has he read than Ted?

Do you add, subtract, multiply, or divide?

How many eggs will fit into a box 12" long and 2" wide?

Can you solve this problem? If not, what do you need to know?

A rectangular field is 9' by 12'. A fence is put around one half of the field. Six feet of fencing is needed for one of the sides. How much is needed for each of the other sides?

Draw a diagram to show your answer.

The high temperature for today was 32° more than the low. If the low temperature was ☐°, what was today's high?

Write the equation. Let N stand for the answer.

(If the low was 45°, can you solve the equation?)

Weekly

Place each number below in one of the blanks to create the most meaningful and realistic story possible.

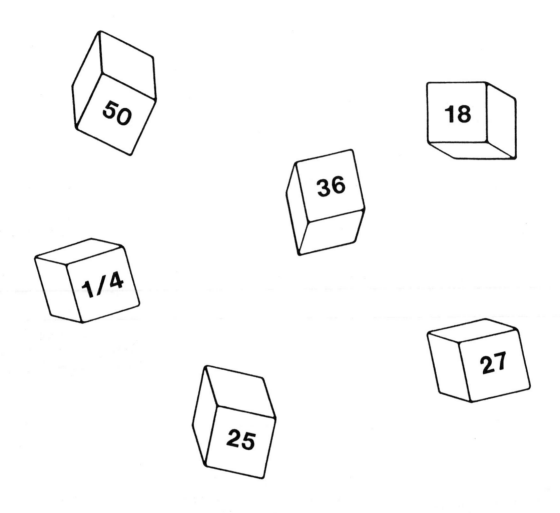

A sweater usually costing $_____ is on sale for _____ off. It now sells for $_____, a savings of _____%. If it was on sale for _____% off, it would only cost $_____, half the original price.

Numbers And Words: A Problem Per Day © 1987 Cuisenaire Company Of America, Inc.

Answers

Page 5
Mon: varies
Tues: multiply
Wed: yes
Thurs:

Fri: 5×□=N; 100

Page 6
Weekly: 3; 35; 60; 2; 105; 7

Page 7
Mon: varies
Tues: subtract
Wed: no; the cost of the hamburger
Thurs:

Fri: (4×□)+95=N; $195

Page 8
Weekly: 3; 4; 12; 2; 1; 24

Page 9
Mon: varies
Tues: add or multiply
Wed: no; what time snack is
Thurs:

Fri: 3×□=N; 15

Page 10
Weekly: 2; 40 or 45; 45 or 40; 1; 15; 3; 5

Page 11
Mon: varies
Tues: multiply or add
Wed: no; how many words she mispelled
Thurs:

Fri: □−($8.00+$1.50)=N; $0.50

Page 12
Weekly: 40; 3; 1.20; 1.80; 6; 3.20; 12; 1

Page 13
Mon: varies
Tues: divide and add
Wed: no; the length of the shoelace

Thurs:

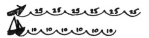

Fri: 100−□=N; 84

Page 14
Weekly: 850; 625; 88; 225; 16; 17

Page 15
Mon: varies
Tues: add
Wed: yes
Thurs:

Fri: 30×□=N; 60

Page 16
Weekly: 3; 8; 6; 4; 2; 1

Page 17
Mon: varies
Tues: divide
Wed: yes
Thurs:

Fri: □−6=N; 59

Page 18
Weekly: 2; 400; 50; 4; 1/2; 200; 8

Page 19
Mon: varies
Tues: subtract
Wed: yes
Thurs:

Fri: 12×□=N; $1.44

Page 20
Weekly: 5; 8; 40; 4; 48; 46; 52

Page 21
Mon: varies
Tues: divide and multiply or add and divide
Wed: yes
Thurs:

Fri: □−13=N; 26

Page 22
Weekly: 90; 85; 5; 40; 50; 10

Page 23
Mon: varies
Tues: multiply
Wed: no; if the water is hotter or colder than the air
Thurs:

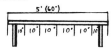

Fri: 1/2×□=N; 12

Page 24
Weekly: 8; 3; 5; 3; 80; 1.20; 6; 1

Page 25
Mon: varies
Tues: subtract
Wed: yes
Thurs:

Fri: 5×□=N; 40

Page 26
Weekly: 10; 4; 25; 50; 85; 15

Page 27
Mon: varies
Tues: divide and multiply
Wed: no; the difference in height between the boys
Thurs:

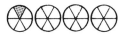

Fri: 256+□=N; $299

Page 28
Weekly: 7; 1/2; 12; 2; 8; 6

Page 29
Mon: varies
Tues: multiply
Wed: yes
Thurs:

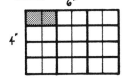

Fri: □+12=N; 30

64

Answers

Page 30
Weekly: 215; 450; 8; 170; 195; 10; 1/2

Page 31
Mon: varies
Tues: divide or multiply
Wed: yes
Thurs:

Fri: □÷6=N; 4

Page 32
Weekly: 3; 3.90; 4.90; 2; 8; 9; 4; 5

Page 33
Mon: varies
Tues: multiply
Wed: yes
Thurs:

Fri: 30+□=N; 40

Page 34
Weekly: 72; 55; 17; 2; 144; 110

Page 35
Mon: varies
Tues: multiply
Wed: no; how many beds per room
Thurs:

Fri: 85+□=N; $105

Page 36
Weekly: 31; 28; 29; 30; 5; 4; 7

Page 37
Mon: varies
Tues: divide
Wed: yes
Thurs:

Fri: 1/2×□=N; 45

Page 38
Weekly: 35; 30; 5; 7; 4; 20; 15

Page 39
Mon: varies
Tues: divide
Wed: yes
Thurs:

Fri: 4+2+□=N; 13

Page 40
Weekly: 6; 18; 12; 4; 2; 1; 5

Page 41
Mon: varies
Tues: multiply, multiply, and subtract or subtract and multiply
Wed: no; what time the store closes
Thurs:

Fri: 90÷□=N; 9

Page 42
Weekly: 18; 8; 1; 2; 9; 4

Page 43
Mon: varies
Tues: subtract
Wed: no; what she had to start with
Thurs:

Fri: □÷12=N; 4

Page 44
Weekly: 2; 30; 4; 1; 3; 60

Page 45
Mon: varies
Tues: add
Wed: yes
Thurs:

Fri: 5×□; 15

Page 46
Weekly: 50; 3; 2; 1; 90; 10; 4; 35

Page 47
Mon: varies
Tues: divide and multiply
Wed: no; the amount she had before the purchase
Thurs:

Fri: .22×□=N; $0.88

Page 48
Weekly: 94; 120; 48; 16; 32; 89; 5

Page 49
Mon: varies
Tues: subtract
Wed: no; if the groups each have the same number of students
Thurs:

Fri: 480−□=N; 230

Page 50
Weekly: 7; 15; 75; 90; 5; 2

Page 51
Mon: varies
Tues: add and multiply
Wed: yes
Thurs:

Fri: 300÷□=N; 100

Page 52
Weekly: 10; 300; 210 or 220; 220 or 210; 200; 100

Page 53
Mon: varies
Tues: add
Wed: no; if each potato weighs the same amount; yes
Thurs:

Fri: 2+5+□=N; 13